Eating
Thistles

Eating Thistles

Deborah Moffatt

Smokestack Books
1 Lake Terrace, Grewelthorpe, Ripon HG4 3BU
e-mail: info@smokestack-books.co.uk
www.smokestack-books.co.uk

Text copyright 2019,
Deborah Moffatt,
all rights reserved.

ISBN 978-1-9996742-9-8

Smokestack Books
is represented
by Inpress Ltd

*There is a road that turning always
Cuts off the country of Again.*
Edwin Muir

Contents

Eating Thistles	11
At Meroe	12
The Accident	16
The Long Game	18
Hunting Caribou	19
Eclogue	21
Cross-roads	22
Missing the Elemental	28
Hostages	36
The Corroding Tide	37
The Gates of Janus	38
Oblivion	40
Hostage to Fortune	41
Glass Houses	42
The Baltic Shore	43
Death in a Public Place	44
Montevideo, 1974	45
The Roman Road	47
Rules of Engagement	49
Hector MacDonald in Paris	50
Fire on the Shore	51
Carmichael in St. Kilda	52
The Innocents	55
The St. Kilda Wren	57
Kitchener in Ireland	58
The Moving Island	59
End-game	61
Along the Coast	62
Floods	63
Of Boats and Bars	64
Out of the Blue	65
They Had a Garden	66
A Change of House	67
Breakdown	68
The Dog-Wifey	69

Dundee Wedding	70
Shallow Land	71
The Neighbour's Buddleia	73
The Marvel of the Parish	74
The Christian Door	75
The New Toboggan	76
Milkweed Down	77
Earthquake	79
Inheritance	81
The Anarchy Waltz	82
Love at the Endings	83
Letter from a Lover Who Doesn't Exist	84
Spring in the Glen	85
Stag	87
The Screen Door	88
The School-teacher's Wife	90
A Distant Island	100
Acknowledgements and Notes	101

Eating Thistles

We ate thistles, and spoke a language
as sharp and barbed as the wire on their walls.

We slept on stone, bathed in snow,
made combs from thorns, clothes from nettles.

Words froze on our tongues
and fell in frozen lumps on barren land.

In their cities and in their towns
they gloried in victory, a nation once again.

We heard their pipes and their drums,
gunshot, fireworks, songs of celebration.

Maddened by power, powered by madness,
they closed their borders, then turned against their own.

Better to sleep on stone, however hard,
better to eat thistles, though we choke,

better our frozen silence than their fiery rhetoric,
better thorns and nettles than pomp and glory,

better to die in a barren wilderness
than to survive in a nation born of vanity.

At Meroe

1

Revenge is sweet, it is said, and although we lost
what little we had once won, the Roman garrisons
at Elephantine Island, and Syene and Philae
with their great temples and their slaves,
at least we kept our pride, and gained
later an advantageous peace,

and if only I had not seen that magnificent head
and those bright staring eyes, I could take delight
in the daily humiliation of the great Caesar,
his head wrested from his statue and buried
here beneath my feet, our fleeting victory
enduring, even in defeat.

Yet that same head, that image of the handsome Augustus
as he was when young, his thick curls licking at his brow,
his bronze skin tinged with an olive hue, his tender lips
set for a kiss, his radiant eyes turned contemptuously aside,
as if my dark Nubian skin or my own blighted eye
offended him, or as if I were not worthy of his gaze,

how that image now haunts my dreams and burdens my heart,
and I regret that I did not think to make my enemy my friend,
and that rather than parade my vanity over his severed head
I might instead have lain beneath him in my bed,
his soft lips pressed against mine, his kisses
so much sweeter than revenge.

2

Kitchener was there, standing hand on hip
in the midst of it all, imperious, distant,
his smile a grimace, his eyes straying,
his patience tried, or spent,

unless it was something else: regret,
unease, at the sight of the severed head,
an unwelcome reminder of the Mahdi's skull
taken from the desecrated tomb at Omdurman,

or was it the aspect of that handsome young face,
the skin pickled by time to a sickly green,
the penetrating eyes turned to the side
as if to avoid Kitchener's wayward gaze?

Those squinting British eyes that would soon raise an army,
those piercing Roman eyes that forged an empire,
the unforgiving eyes of a callous youth,
the weary eyes of a tired old man;

through clenched teeth, Kitchener sighs
and silently grieves for the young lives
of men, his band of boys, lost
to the passage of time.

3

It is too late. The cloud of tobacco smoke
drifting through the cab, the terrible choke
of diesel fumes, the driver's manic laughter,
the squalling radio: it all belongs to another time.

Like rotten teeth on an old jawbone,
truncated pyramids stud the horizon.
The driver is ranting, the guide suspicious.
Your companions talk in code, trusting no one.

The road to Meroe was built by Bin Laden,
your hotel by Gaddafi: everything here is history.
The guide eyes your wedding rings with contempt;
even your marriage belongs to the past.

The one-eyed warrior Queen, the severed head
of an emperor, a nation divided, its heritage
endangered: there is a story here,
but it isn't the one you've come to find.

Your companions tap at their phones, waiting
for news to break. You scan the desert sky,
looking for a change in the weather, an avatar,
the emperor's head, suspended in time.

There is something stubborn, implacable,
about those lips, as if it were all your fault,
not his, and a sadness in those eyes,
avoiding yours every time he lied.

You shouldn't have come, but it's too late
now, for regrets. One after another
they were lost: colleagues, friends, lovers.
Nobody ever said, enough is enough.

The truck rumbles over Bin Laden's road. Revenge
is impossible. There was never anyone to blame.
A moment of carelessness, and you die.
At least he didn't lie when he said goodbye.

The Accident

A shadow remains,
an absence of clarity,
a day that never brightens,
a dusk that won't resolve into night.

They ask, how did you do it,
not, how did it happen,
as if it were all your fault,
this accident of history.

It might have been Dublin or Derry,
or Boston or Chicago,
a bullet, or a fist, or the kiss
of the cold hard ground.

Your blood was soiled, stained
the rusty red of corrugated iron,
the orange-black of the bog,
dirt and blood, metal and bone.

The amber glow on the peatlands
and the green on the cottage door
offer a welcome as deceptive
as the flickering light on the shore.

You were left with a numb jaw,
the insensitivity of a cheek
you never learned to turn
until it was too late.

And in your ears, a constant crackling,
as of bullets fired or fists slamming
or feet tapping unevenly on a hard floor,
the unsteady steps of old men dancing.

You never did notice the pain.
Paralysed by fear, or pride,
you kept on smiling, and lied,
about everything.

The Long Game

until you have killed
a heron a raven
and a deer
you are not a hunter

how they laugh!
the rutting deer snorts
the nesting heron coughs
the raven prophesies

hand to mouth
river to river
mud and bog
cold and hunger

the shaking hand
the squint in the eye
the errant shot
dissemblance

let them laugh
yours the bog
the decadence
the long game

Hunting Caribou

Batiste stares at the stony ridge, his eyes steady.
If you look for them, he says, you will never see them.
Every boulder you will mistake for caribou,
every twig for their horns.

At the bottom of the ridge a river flows, drawing your eye
wide across the miles of barren ground to the frozen north.
You look for a shudder of light, a sudden shadow,
a hint of change in an immutable landscape.

Yellow smoke drifts over the sun, darkening the day.
A velvet haze softens the intensity of Batiste's eyes.
'We wait,' he says, as if that needed to be said,
as if there were anything else to do.

Batiste doesn't know you. You've seen the caribou,
already, in the shake of a twig, in a boulder, dislodged.
You wait. Half a lifetime you've spent
learning to be invisible.

Missing, presumed dead, a mother's blue-eyed son,
long gone, lost or strayed: you are the caribou,
the dormant boulder, the resting twig.
People see what they want to see.

The purple sun hangs low above the ridge; time drags.
Batiste never looks at you, only sniffs, now and then,
as if to catch your scent. You wonder when
he was last 'outside,' if ever he was.

After all those years of hiding in plain sight, here you are,
in a wilderness, gun in hand. Batiste doesn't trust you,
that's clear. You've never needed to use a gun before.
You found other ways to survive.

One shot, and the caribou scatter, easy prey. Batiste laughs.
You move closer to him, taking no chances.
Between the hunter and the hunted,
every shot counts.

Eclogue

Here in the north it rains a lot,
but you can always fish, and drink tea,
cups of tea all through the day,

and always the rain is falling lightly on the lough,
the tiny drops distressing the surface,
giving definition to the dull grey water,

the still water on a rainy day, the afternoon
strewn with cups of tea, the occasional fish,
leaping, mouth gaping, for the fly,

the fish lured by the fly to their death,
fish and fly and death and rain
defining the long days,

the snap of the rod, the whisper of the line,
the ripples in the water, the hiss of the kettle,
the constant kiss of rain on your face,

the whispers of warning, the smarting snap
of danger in the wind, the contrary flags
waving boldly at either end of the street,

the gaily-painted kerbstones, the villages and towns
defined by their colours, a landscape distressed
by gaping holes in buildings and roads,

the long afternoons, strewn with cups of tea and tears
at funerals and bedsides, in hospitals and courtrooms,
guns and bombs defining a nation;

but you can always fish, here in the north, and drink tea
laced with whiskey, and you can always pray
that tomorrow it will not rain.

Crossroads

i   Crossroads

At every crossroad there is a pub,
and on every hill a church.
On every side of every road, there is a ditch,
and beyond each ditch, a hedge,
and behind the hedge a field,
and in every field, cows,
or sheep, or a horse,
or maybe a pig or two.

I know it all so well.
In those damp fields
I've cut hay and dug potatoes.
I've milked those cows,
shorn those sheep, ridden the horse,
sat for hours on a Sunday
in a cold and cheerless church,
then, later, eaten the neighbour's pig.

In a warm convivial pub
on a Saturday,
I've drunk too much brandy,
stumbled home
along these narrow roads,
caught my coat on a prickly hedge,
strayed from the road,
lain in a ditch until dawn.

ii Unfinished Business

Once only did I leave a job undone – a cross
on an island in Lough Erne, when I was young,
I never finished – but I had reason enough for that,
with all the disruptions, the constant invasions,
Devenish, and Clones, and all the churches on the lough
destroyed by the marauders from the north,
the fair foreigners with eyes the colour of ice
and a genius for organisation, who left behind
a legacy of construction, for all the damage done,
a legacy that lured me south to the great new towns,
hard though it was to leave the land of my birth
and the dark rippling waters of Lough Erne.

That cross I left, unfinished, after many long hours
spent alone, the stone silent and sturdy, the pattern
slow to emerge, little to show for all my work
at the end of a day. It was when I saw the holy men
with their pens fill a page with a lifetime of thoughts
in the space of an hour and then, with a bit of pigment
and a flick of a brush, add colour to illuminate
the delicate tracery round every letter, while I
for every curve of every line worked arduously,
day after day, and when I heard of the marvels
of the southern towns, where labour and leisure
and commerce and conversation abound, while for me
the only pleasure to be found was in quiet contemplation
of the beautiful dark waters of Lough Erne,

then, I put down my hammer and chisel and went away,
with few regrets. Although that cross, unfinished,
haunts me yet, for all that I was impatient when young,
beguiled by change and all that was new; now, older,
wiser, perhaps, with time to spare yet little time left,
and knowing that nothing lasts forever, I nevertheless
would happily spend the rest of my days labouring
at snail's pace on one small bit of stone, to know
the contentment of a job well done, God's work
completed in peace and contentment, there
by the dark still waters of Lough Erne.

iii Crossroads

Sure I saw it in the animals, often enough,
that pointless desire for change, no matter
how green the grass, how sweet the water,
how sheltered the field in stormy weather.
Something better, they imagined, was out there
beyond the prickly hedges and barbed wire fences
that held them captive, the new, the different,
the unknown always more attractive than the known.

iv Sir John Hume at Tully Castle

When first I came to Tully
I thought I could never learn to love it.
I missed the icy clarity of the winter sunlight
on the silver waters of the Forth,
the bracing burst of the cold east wind,
the bruised darkness of the evening sky
beyond Edinburgh's tall spires.

Here the light is dull, softened at all times
by a residue of dampness, Lough Erne
a sullen grey more often than not,
the sky more nearly white than blue,
the breeze cloying with a faint reminiscence
of the Atlantic, the brackish air
settling fine as silk on the skin.

Yet it is that same dampness,
that softness, the subtle beauty of grey,
that enchants me now;
and for all the threats I hear
of trouble and unrest on all sides,
I would not be tempted to leave this place,
not for gold, not for my King, not for God.

v Crossroads

Ruins, relics, remnants, clutter the map:
here a holy well, there a Mass rock,
everywhere raths, on Inishmacsaint
a half-finished cross, at Tully
a ransacked castle.

But you would never need to look at a map;
you know it all so well: this place, this past.

At the cross-roads, you linger, and listen:
in a distant field cattle are lowing,
a choir practices in the church on the hill,
through the open door of the pub on the corner
melodies escape – the Maho Snaps, the Noone Lasses.

From here, it's all the same, wherever you go:
four roads for leaving, four roads for returning.

Missing the Elemental

a St. Kilda Triad

1

Is this how it is, then, to be on the cusp of extinction, life
becoming death, flesh and bone dust, memory fading to myth,

just this, a pompous little bird on a plinth, up-right, ungainly,
clumsy on land, strong in the water, out of place, out of time,

and you, on the other side of the glass case, weak, alone,
lost in the whispering hollows of the vast museum,

the rustle of coats, the shuffle of shoes, the rumours,
imagined or real, nowhere to hide but inside the glass

closing mercilessly around you, extinguishing what little is left
of all that you once were, the last of your kind?

2

As soon as he arrives he would rather be leaving,
and leaving, will keep his back to the island
his eyes on the sea, heading east, *an ear,*

into tomorrow and the day after, *an earar,*
leaving behind the west, *an àirde an iar air a chùl,*
never looking back at the setting sun

as if it were a curse or a sin to remember the past
or to remain too long among the abandoned ruins
or to ask a question that has no answer.

3

The end of the world, should it come, will be foretold,
a blip on a screen, a frantic pit-pit-pit on a monitor,
the disordered heart-beat of time running out;
here on the base, we know everything, and nothing at all.

Our eyes on the screen, we watch for the incidental
and miss the elemental, the caress of the wind on our skin,
the blinding glare of the sun on the water,
the ceaseless susurration of the waves on the shore.

4

He waits until the last passenger alights on the island –
these travellers who have come here to see
what is no longer here to be seen,

who search for clues to the past in dust and ash,
in bones and stones, in fragments of story and song,
inspired by the romance of all that is lost,

by the tantalizing uncertainty of what can only be imagined,
or reconstructed, or supposed, or invented,
but never truly known.

5

What we can't see and don't know is what matters:
a Sunderland flying boat buried somewhere in the glen,
its crew of ten scattered at sea, and with them an eleventh body,
an unofficial casualty, never identified, never acknowledged,

a death as much a mystery as that of the great auk,
killed, the story goes, by the islanders themselves,
mistaken for a witch, bludgeoned or stoned to death,
the last of its kind to ever be seen on these islands.

6

Impossible now to separate the truth from the lie, if ever it was,
mas breug bhuam e, or to know what might have been said
or done, *is breug thugam e,* for a lump of tobacco or a bit of fun.

7

The deceit, the lies, the stories told; eyes on the floor,
they pass you by, whispering, rustling, judging: they know.

It wasn't necessarily a lie. To destroy what you loved,
what you needed most in life: that could happen.

In every Gaelic proverb there were always three of a kind,
and you imagine the distant points of a triangle: you, here,

and a man on a train, heading homewards, to the highlands
and his wife, knowing that three into two won't go.

Excuses are made: a bird was killed for a witch,
witches were burnt at a stake. You long for escape,

but there is nowhere to go, nowhere left to hide, all eyes staring
as you lean close to the glass to kiss the flightless bird good-by.

8

One day, he knows, he will set sail and never return,
abandoning his passengers on the abandoned island,
his past becoming their future, his story their destiny.

Hostages

In the middle of the night the phone rang:
someone had seen a falling star.
We had bartered tomorrow for today,
gambled, and lost.

You went out to the garden
and lay naked in a nettle bed.
There were sacrifices to be made.
People looked the other way.

You were the first to fall. One by one,
they took us all. Now the phone
never rings; not a star
is left in the sky.

The Corroding Tide

pillar of light
stacking high on the horizon

ice on the shore,
the arid blue-grey
of old woman skin
on cold bone

want and waste
nothing was ever saved

an insolent spire
pricks the sullen sky
reason fades
light disintegrates

black dawn
another night lost

the corroding tide
chafes the crusty shore
an ululation of desire
the old whore tongue

waste and want
nothing lasts

The Gates of Janus

'[Janus] has a temple at Rome with double doors, which they call the gates of war; for the temple always stands open in time of war, but is closed when peace has come. The latter was a difficult matter, and it rarely happened...'
Plutarch

You, love, standing braced in the doorway, arms out-stretched,
hands firm against the door-frame, your head bowed, crowned
with thorns of grief and despair, your chest torn and bruised,
blood weeping from your wounds, a martyr to a lost cause,
trying to stop the passage of time, suspended
between the old year and the new,
between this life and the next,
this hell, this earth.

In the shadows, the children lie sprawled in a nest of rags,
twig-thin limbs jutting from disfigured trunks, bony wrists
and sharp elbows, gnarled knees and twisted ankles,
cracked lips and pock-marked faces all hidden
in shame, as if hunger were a disgrace,
and pain a punishment, their innocence
stolen, traded for whatever it takes
to survive these dying days.

An old woman rocks in a corner, drones an endless prayer,
O death where, her eyes white with age, blinded by faith,
where is thy sting, and waits in an ecstasy of mourning
for a prophecy that will never come to pass, *o grave*,
her eyes bright with an inner light, *where*,
with a vision that only she can see,
the mystery of immortality;
where is they victory?

While I stand beside a window, in full view of the snipers' eyes,
longing to feel your fingers entwined in my hair one last time,
your lips on mine, a final kiss as rockets flare and bonfires burn
and drums beat and bullets sing, war masquerading as peace
amid the rising smoke and the falling ash, a celebration
of transition, *death*, of the opening of a gate, the end
of this temporal life, the promise of eternity,
swallowed up in victory.

Oblivion

A child dangles from a twisted rope,
spins himself stupid as the rope unwinds,
staggers with a gaping grin down the sloping grass.

At a window in a house near-by a woman stands
and watches the child, while at a piano inside the house
someone practices Bach with careless diligence,
playing the same few notes over and over again.

The woman remembers the dizzy oblivion of childhood,
the hours spent in a mindless daze at the piano,
the countless nights when she danced until dawn,
the days when only alcohol could deaden the pain,
a time when she had been better left for dead.

The child's gaping grin thins to a sickly grimace.
The rope swings idly in a gentle breeze.
The Bach is abandoned; a radio blares.
The woman paces the floor from window to door.

Survival brought a terrible clarity, real life
in all its intensity: everything now matters;
not a thing can be forgotten, or ignored.

Hostage to Fortune

One day, the past saunters into the garden,
bringing memories of all those old difficulties,
the nettles we thought we had eradicated years ago,
the terrifying calls at midnight, the random falling stars.

Now you've come back, ten years late, a vision of the future
even before the present has passed, prematurely aged,
your wild beauty gone, ravaged by illness, not time,
by an inability to live today before tomorrow.

It was Iraq, back then, now Syria, shadow fighting shadow,
layer upon layer of unfathomable darkness, a drifting haze
of chemicals and dust rising from rubble and ash, the nettles
still burning our backs, the future returning to haunt the past.

Glass Houses

They were building the conservatory that summer,
and every morning she made a visit to the site,
looked up through a filigree of thin timber
framing an infinity of light.

He sat all day in the dark, staring at a computer screen,
exploring the internet, the world growing ever nearer,
ever more intimate, as e-mails flew between strangers
and digital imagery left nothing unseen.

We saw the photographs in all the papers:
our soldiers, behaving disgracefully,
posing shamelessly for the ubiquitous cameras,
witlessly betraying the dirty secrets of war.

In the transparent splendour of the conservatory
they entertained, that autumn: he, a mole
blinking shyly in the light; she, over-exposed,
glowing with a dangerous radiance.

Tonight, stars spangle the sky, illuminating little.
Pixels dance uselessly across a darkening screen.
He imagines a great romance where none exists,
while she sits alone in the fading light.

The Baltic Shore

She dresses for dinner beside the meagre fire,
each garment a layer of the past, the faded silk blouse,
the threadbare woollen skirt, the thin cashmere shawl.

You remember the jagged ice floes cluttering the winter sea,
the pale bloated corpses floating like buoys amid the ice,
the ragged clothing flapping wildly in the wind.

Music drifts into the room, a Haydn quartet, stately and sweet,
the music of vanished empires and vanquished nations,
of displacement and exile, disruption and confusion.

You remember gunshots in the mine, bodies buried in the sand,
the few survivors wandering in the street, half-mad,
memories you weren't allowed to have.

The room smells of neglect, the ageing immigrant a burden
to her hosts, her welcome worn thin as the clothes on her back,
her only consolation the golden glow at the heart of the fire.

After a storm you would find the nuggets on the shore,
small pebbles nestled in twigs, soft to the touch, electric
when rubbed, alive with an ancient fire, a beam of the sun.

She finds a necklace in a box, rests the amber stone in her hand
as if to weigh the past, inspects the insect preserved within,
evidence of history that cannot be denied.

The war was lost, and won. The Jews were reburied, renamed
as Soviet heroes, their faith buried with them in their graves,
rumour and myth giving way to secrecy and lies.

Beside the dying fire, she waits for the final call.
Outside, a moon shines blue on snow and ice, layers
of silence separating her forever from that distant Baltic shore.

Death in a Public Place

On the terrace of a café, they sit in weary silence,
sipping strong coffee in the warm afternoon sun,
lulled by the dull hum of the constant traffic,
the busy street half-hidden by a veil of reek
glistening with an insidious iridescence.

In a secluded corner of a tree-lined park
a young woman idly minds a quiet child,
the child lost in play, the woman lost in a dream,
the rustling leaves whispering promises in her ear,
the child's sudden screams unheeded.

At the centre of it all a tall young man with a wild eye
dominates a crowded pavement, marching to the drum
of his own band, an army of one, sensing victory,
he the soul of this land, its future and its past, an avatar
forever fighting a war with no beginning and no end.

Not even he is prepared for what happens next,
the sudden eruption of violence, death in a public place,
on the steps of a museum, bullets and bodies and blood,
innocents inexplicably gunned down in broad daylight.
The sirens scream. He runs for his life, hides in a park

where the young woman squats beside a gurgling fountain,
rocking her terrified child in her arms, the babbling water
whispering in a strange language she can't understand,
her confusion promising a future of anger and resentment,
a baptism of fear raining down over the child's head.

On the terrace of the city café there is an exhalation of relief,
colour returning to pale cheeks, 'nothing to do with us.'
The word goes round, 'just Israelis and Arabs, spies, *Juifs*.'
They sit in silence, his hand concealing her Antwerp diamond.
It is never, they know, nothing to do with them.

Montevideo, 1974

We meet in a hotel of convenience: an inconspicuous entrance,
money paid at the door, a small dark room, a bed and little else,
enough, for us, these few hours together all we have left.

The city is deserted, stripped bare. Not even a shadow
darkens the empty streets, nothing but the unwavering glare
of repression in a nation paralysed by fear.

Pale men in elegant suits slip invisibly through city streets,
hide inside dark cafés, drink strong coffee and weak whisky,
and argue, theatrically, impotently, for hours, about nothing.

In the *barrios*, beautiful women hardened by poverty
march with grim determination to the weekly market,
intent on buying what they know will not be there.

At night in the *boliches* there are only fools and old men:
those who are above the law or beneath contempt,
the innocent, the corrupt, the survivors, the damned.

In that drab little room we come alive, lips meeting lips,
the soft stroke of a finger-tip eliciting salt-sweet secretions,
the intimacy of penetration, the tenderness of skin on skin.

In a prison called *Libertad*, the living are left for dead,
alone in windowless cells, a solitary light-bulb overhead
burning all meaning from their minds.

We tear each other apart, rub every membrane raw, stumble
and flail, fall and crawl, the room a battlefield, our memories
our enemy, until we are certain: nothing can hurt us now.

Everyone is leaving this beautiful country, this Switzerland
of the south. He holds a cigarette between his broken fingers,
studies the smoke as if it were a map, as if it were a rope.

Out on the street we say good-bye, and go our separate ways. Broken hands, broken hearts, live or die, it hardly matters; the damage is done. For the last time, we say good-bye.

The Roman Road

He savours his solitude, the long hours alone in a quiet room,
the computer humming quietly on the desk, the pale screen
bright with promise, the open books, the bits of paper,
the scribbled notes, page after page of research,
of preparation, of contemplation, the flare of a match,
a silver curl of smoke, a quick cigarette at the open window,
the sudden ping of an incoming e-mail offering a diversion,
a chance correspondence, the possibility of a casual romance.

Imagine *architectus,* he writes, a man with an eye for the land,
with a vision to transform this trackless wilderness,
to tame this spiteful earth, to fell these trees,
to drain these wetlands, to divert these streams,
to dig and hollow the soil, to pack and ram a *gremium*,
a reliable bed that will not give way,
to build a road, long and straight and true:
Empire's penetrating arrow.

She remembers the road, a wash of green on either side,
the supple limbs of the young trees bending low over her,
the gentle touch of their hands, tenderly consoling her
in the long green corridor, wheels spinning freely,
her future reeling out before her, straight and true,
the beguiling possibilities, their strong hands restraining her,
the driving headstrong along that silver ribbon of road
into the constantly receding promise of the pale morning light.

He endures his solitude, takes pleasure in the neat black lines,
the first hesitant threads of a narrative unreeling on the screen,
the hours of contemplation interspersed with a fury of typing,
the chattering keyboard a scold, a reminder of work to be done,
while e-mails remain unanswered and romance is postponed,
the trajectory of his life as oblique as that of the tales he tells,
though he never loses sight of what lies ahead, the threads
left dangling, the thrill of the conquest, the promise of success.

The road that autumn was not as she had remembered it,
the light darker, foreboding, the trees older, stiff, unforgiving,
the tarnished leaves stubbornly bright against the dull sky,
the silver road faded to grey, slick with a mist of rain, or tears,
or blood, and somewhere in the mist a face, indistinct, appears
at the side of the road, a possible diversion, one last chance,
a yearning, a moment's indecision, but how, they whisper now,
could anyone possibly go astray on a road so straight and true?

His work nearly done, he regrets his solitude, frets over emails
that no longer arrive, senses her pain and blames himself,
though it was never just a simple matter of building a road,
he writes, not only the earth that was unreliable – even history
could not be trusted, Calgacus a rhetorical device, a construct,
Mons Graupius a myth, a victory claimed but never won,
a peace, of sorts, declared, as light fades from the screen,
leaving a solitary thread of smoke dangling in an empty room.

Rules of Engagement

No one wins this dangerous game,
this dance of opposing forces.

A glance that lingers a second too long,
a hand that strays too close to the flesh,

an unwarranted warmth: it might be love,
it might be war. We know the rules.

A step too far, the wire trips; everyone loses
when there is nothing left to be won.

Hector MacDonald in Paris

Eyes to the front, shoulders back, he marches – *forward!* –
straight as an arrow through the scattered tables,
the room an imagined battlefield, every man a soldier
drilled to perfection, even here, even now – *mark time!* –
    every man on parade, unto the end.

Ah but these French lads are a careless lot,
their minds filled with the insignificant thoughts
of civilian life, with bread and circuses, not war,
these young men so alive with music and dance,
    the tender young men, so full of grace.

He eats his breakfast with precision, his hands steady
on fork and knife, hands long skilled in the use of weapons,
though the casual savagery of war is as alien to him still
as the gentle kindness of love or the softness of women,
    the terrifying softness of kind women.

Breakfast over, time moves pointlessly on, the long day
yawning, the war nearly over, the battlefield disintegrating,
his expertise in the geometry of war of little use to him now,
here in the drawing room of a Paris hotel, this his last retreat,
    where he reads the words that will seal his fate.

He prepares his death with that same diligent precision,
empties his pockets, tucks his boots neatly beneath the bed,
stands tall before the mirror, takes aim at himself, he the enemy,
he the executioner, a man condemned and killed by his own hand,
    this great leader of men, in command unto the end.

Fire on the Shore

Up here there is a mist so thick I can barely see my hand;
down there, a fire on the shore, red flames rising,
rage burning hot beneath a smothering sky.

I know the lie of the land, every hedge, every tree,
every wall, every gate, but still, in a mist like this
everything looks strange – a man could easily go astray.

I never have: every furrow I ever ploughed, every dreel,
straight as a die, and never a hint of trouble from me;
no harm did I ever do to any man or beast.

Here I am with nothing to call my own, and little to show
for a good man's life but my name on a slab of stone
when I'm gone, though I never asked for more.

I trusted the laird and the promises he made,
and held my tongue when others were betrayed
by his broken promises and his lies.

By God it's cold now in this mist, though I can't complain.
My voice silenced by acquiescence, dumb and damp
as these poor cows, I wander lost in a thickening fog.

But that's a braw fire down there on the shore,
and wouldn't the laird warm himself with his ire
if he knew they had used his boat-house to kindle their fire.

Carmichael in St. Kilda

See there, that island, a wee skelp of land abandoned mid-sea,
a solid lump of grey rock and green grass, boulders and scree,
rising boldly through a drift of mist into an eternity of sky,
a froth of white foam fringing the shores of the bay
between the smooth slopes of Oiseabhal
and the jagged arm of the Dùn;

and down there, a line of low houses set back from the shore,
tiled roofs and white chimneys bright in the morning sun,
taighean geala, built on this island well before their time –
does anyone among the crowd, newly-landed on the shore,
the sea still rocking the ground beneath their unsteady feet,
notice, now, this anomaly, this anachronism?

The young exciseman with keen eyes, zealously taking notes,
here to collect not taxes but tales, the chronicler of the Gaels –
he notices it all, records all he sees, the handsome women,
their high shoulders, their good teeth, their crouched figures
and bad feet, and the men, pale and stout, spoiled, he writes,
not polite, and the barking dogs, mad with with excitement,

the entire village mad with excitement, the minister frets,
himself only recently arrived and uncertain, still, of his flock,
as nervously he pats his rumpled waist-coat, checks the time,
plucks his watch from its pocket then dips it back in again,
rueing the disorder, the confusion, the beguiling intrusion
of outsiders who will not understand the nature of the island.

The two men meet on the shore, the fervent minister Mackay
and the tenacious collector Carmichael, both determined,
each with a mission to complete, one with souls to save,
the other a precious heritage to preserve, one wary, one warm,
the minister fearful that old memories of the foolish past
should be stirred, Carmichael not likely to be deterred,

and before long he finds his way unerringly to his source,
the very woman he has come here to meet, the aged cottar
who carries the traditions, the stories, the songs, in her head,
but not before he has stopped to kiss a lassie, a little beauty,
kissed her to say that he has kissed a St. Kilda lassie,
the collector of stories creating a story of his own to tell,

another St. Kilda story among the rest, tales of love and loss,
is tu mo luran, is tu mo leannan, of courting and death,
of dangerous cliffs and fatal falls, the harvesting of birds
and the sea's harvest of lives, *Tì gad chaomhnadh,
dùl gad chomhnadh,* the harvest of stories and songs
that Carmichael eagerly reaps from Oighrig NicCruimein,

and she, welcoming and strong-minded – come in, *a laochain* –
has drawn him in from the noise of the people and the dogs,
this man with his paper and his pens and an ear for a song,
old stories and songs not heard on this island these long years,
silenced, now, by piety, by censure or by consent, yet still,
alive – *cluinneam an ceòl!* – in the old woman's memory,

the music and dance not yet consigned to the past,
the songs of birds returning to the cliffs, the men dancing
on the end of a long rope high above the sea, a fearful sight,
Carmichael writes, but, for us, she tells him, it is all the same,
the fear and the joy, the music and the dance, work and play,
buidheachas dhan Tì, thàinig na gugachan, united by faith;

for how, without faith, would we have survived this hard life,
she asks, and though now she delights in singing her songs
and telling her tales, does she nevertheless regret the piety
that has silenced her past, or is it the past itself that she regrets,
and the re-awakening in her mind of those innocent pastimes
which now have no place in the grace of her soul?

And neither is Carmichael without regrets, his visit spoiled
by the rabble in the streets and the interfering minister, a legacy
lost, a heritage that will die on the lips of the dying woman,
Oighrig NicCruimein dead before his return, little to show
for his time on the island but a song of undying love
gaol nach claon gun tèid mi 's talamh and a kiss.

The Innocents

The children are out in the fields again,
their golden heads bobbing between the rows of barley,
for all the times they've been told keep away from the corn.

We were young, frightened, cold, poor;

If they don't watch there'll be a row. But they won't watch –
children don't. They have no idea of trouble before it comes.
But if they look this way – and they do, they see me here,
waving to them, and they will know, everyone knows,
I've never turned a child away hungry from this door.

they were neighbours, friends.

Aye, always something here for them, their greedy wee hands
grabbing at my apron, their cheeks puffed with sweets.
Pleased with their good fortune, they never notice
my hands running through their tousled hair,
picking out the tell-tale bits of chaff.

We were made to take the gold from their teeth,

Though it hardly matters what the children do,
their play no worse for the crops than the farmers' labour,
the incessant ploughing stripping the goodness from the land;

and forced to dig deep pits for their graves.

you'd think the farmers would learn from their mistakes,
though I don't suppose anyone ever learns
or pays much attention to the lessons of the past,
and certain things are best forgotten, or never mentioned,
or perhaps it's just that questions are never asked.

We never told a soul, never said a word,

We are getting older now, though, and the past,
when we die, will die with us, and when the ploughs
unearth old bones in those fields, as they so often do,
there will be no one left who knows whose bones they were,
or how they came to be buried there.

not a word about the rivers of blood, the graves that stirred,
the warm bodies that we trampled with our cold bare feet –
as if our silence could make us believe that it never happened.

Ah well, it's time I sent the children home,
their mouths stopped with sweets, their pockets
full of treats, their hair and jumpers plucked clean.
Wee devils, scarpering off without a thought for me;
they're not half as innocent as I would like them to be.

The St. Kilda Wren

Seldom a day when the wren would not be heard on the island,
the incessant chatter and trill, the churr of alarm, the little bird
never silent, you could say, if silence didn't bring to mind
a village, abandoned, if never didn't sound like forever.

On the Dùn and Mullach Bì you would see the wren, tail cocked,
wings whirring, slipping shyly into every nook and cranny,
boldly picking insects from the carcasses of sea bird and fish,
or taking refuge from the cold, or preparing at night to roost.

The king of the birds, the wren, riding high on the eagle's back,
and clever with it, there on the island as much as anywhere else,
surviving against the odds, adapting, over time, a stronger bill,
a paler plumage, larger eggs, evolution a trick of nature,

a trick we never learned, or understood, as others misunderstood
how we had been shaped as much by the nature of our humanity
as by the exigencies of nature. And now we are gone forever
from the island, and only the wren remains to sing our song.

Kitchener in Ireland

There was the day when you lay helpless on the damp grass,
pinned like Gulliver by your brother to the ground,
hostage to the random cruelty of children at play,
a game of croquet gone wrong,

and patiently you waited until someone came, your mother,
plucking at the hoops and clucking in your ear,
stroking your bruised skin and soothing your pride,
trying desperately to look into your wayward eye;

'I don't mind,' you said, and you didn't. A lesson learned.
like all the others: your father's rages, your mother's sighs,
your tutor's contempt, the mocking boys at Banna strand
luring you deeper into the dangerous waves,

a child's play becoming the life of a man, the landed estate
and the men who worked on it set to be your first command,
every field surveyed, drained, known to you by name,
the road laid from Ireland to Omdurman,

until the dampness of the grass crept deep into your heart,
your mother delicately coughing blood in the garden shrubs,
the waves on that distant beach beating a retreat,
the estate sold, Ireland lost, your first defeat.

The Moving Island

It was a desolate island, without trees, without grass.
On a shore without sand we ran the boat aground, and there
on the boat the man of God remained, no fool he, while we,
in vigil and prayer, passed the night on the barren island.

She saw the island as she wanted it to be,
saw beauty in the silver-black water of the lochs,
in the violet-grey grasses of the bogs,
in the cold blue stone of the hill-tops,
in the amber warmth of a man's eyes,
in the bottles lining the shelf above a bar.

In the morning, after Mass, we took all we had from the boat,
the raw meat, salt for the flesh, the few necessities left to us
on our quest to find the blessed island, the promised land,
our Holy Father's will our own, our bodies in his hands.

More than a life on the island, she wanted the island
to be her life, wanted to be defined by the pebbled shores,
the rocky cliffs, the bare hills, the long winding roads,
the remote bothies, the silent men, the wind in her hair, the bog
at her feet, the red-brown murk of peat staining her bare skin,
drawing her in, pulling her deep into the heart of the island.

With the few bits of driftwood that we found we built a fire
and set a pot to boil, and as the flames began to rise higher,
we felt a strange unease, the ground heaving beneath our feet,
the island moving in a great wave from one end to the other.

She wanted too much, tried too hard. She made mistakes,
misjudged the depths, the distances, the solidity of the rocks,
the liquidity of time, the warmth of a man's eyes. From end
to end of the island, silences stretched, certainties slipped,
and through an empty glass she saw what she had missed –
the instability of the island, the subsidence of trust.

*Stricken with terror, we ran from the island, our hearts
full of doubt, our faith sorely tested – for it wasn't lost on us
that our Holy Father had never left the boat, that all along
he must have known what sort of island it was.*

As she tethered her clothes to a rope in a howling wind,
she heard in the distance the music of the pipes, a slow march,
the lop-sided beat of the retreat, and felt stray notes falling
like tears on her face, or perhaps it was the wind she heard,
the rain on her face, the piper and his music only a memory
she was preparing to have after she had left the island.

As we set sail, we saw the island moving away from us,
as if the island had a life of its own that could never be hers,
our poor fire still burning on the creature's scaly back,
as if it had turned its back on her, smoke rising from the hills
the fire we had started in ignorance and desperation,
in silent reproach, as if she were to blame for the damage done,
to satisfy our needs, never thinking of the harm we did,
the eroding trust, the deceptive welcome of an unstable island,
never imagining that God's will would one day lead us astray.
the transient passions at the bottom of an empty glass.

End-Game

It begins one summer evening in a country garden,
a flood of golden light streaming through tall thin trees,
settling like honey on the pale green grass.

Between the shadow and the light, the black and the green,
young men strike languid poses, rarely speaking, barely moving,
pawns in a game whose rules no-one remembers.

In an upstairs bedroom, she lies in the dark,
listening to the dangerous silence of the men in the garden,
watching dust dance in a single beam of light.

Along the thin yellow line that separates green from black
she traces a random route across a tartan blanket,
a map of a long-forgotten land.

As the sky fades from blue to grey a fisherman at sea
studies the stars with an experienced eye,
learning nothing he doesn't already know.

The greater mystery is what he has left behind,
the shifting black shadow on the horizon,
a green land drifting dangerously into uncharted water.

Along The Coast

All along the coast the young men lie in lonely rooms
listening for the welcoming sighs of women lying alone
behind doors left half-closed along darkened landings
on wet dreary nights in the long hours between the last drink
and the break of day, a woman's sigh inviting the young men
to roam from room to room, from bed to bed, from lips to breast
to thighs, to the wine-drenched oblivion of passionless sex
that helps to pass the lonely night somewhere along the coast.

All along the coast the young men die a little every day,
their lives slipping away in the hours spent tending bars
or grooming greens, time spent waiting, watching, dreaming
of possibilities that might arise, or rueing the chances missed,
listening to tales of other men's successes, tales retold, later,
as their own, or listening to bored women in lonely rooms
who know better than to hope for anything more than this,
a night of passion in a dreary room somewhere along the coast.

All along the coast young boys with their fathers' faces
dream of becoming the men their fathers might have been
as their lonely mothers take other men to their beds
on wet dreary nights in the long hours between the last drink
and the start of another day, while young men growing older
sleep alone in rented rooms, their youth spent, their time gone,
every dream abandoned, every penny wasted, every chance
missed, young lives squandered and lost, all along the coast.

Floods

For days it rained. Swollen rivers burst their banks.
Mud and slime oozed through towns.
Roads disintegrated; bridges collapsed.

You sat alone on a stool by the bar
drinking dry martinis, your smile
as wide as the Sahara.

They made their way across the river,
arms and legs flailing, and flopped, belly-down,
spent, on the muddy banks on the far side.

Men drowned their sorrows in beer;
the tears of women sparkled
diamond-bright on powder-dry cheeks.

You've seen it all: natural disasters
and human folly, floods of tears,
the inane babble of gushing laughter.

Let them wallow in the mud, then,
seeking salvation on the other side
while you sit there, drouthy and dry-eyed.

Of Boats and Bars

There were bars, on the island,
and boats, more bars than boats,
beginning in Finnegan's, for lunch,
beer, for the adults, ginger ale, for us,
cigarette smoke clouding the afternoon,
the promise of the boat receding.

Between bars, there were boats,
entire days spent sailing on the Sound,
drinks on board around the wheel, for them,
while we, drunk on sea-spray and strong sun,
sat on the heeling deck, our legs dangling down
over the water, feet skimming the rising waves.

At night, there were discs of green phosphorus
floating in the dark water, and above the harbour
the neon lights of restaurants and bars: more drinks,
Scotch, for them, ice cream with Crème de Menthe, for us,
and at a piano, a man crooning love songs, sultry looks
burning through wreaths of smoke, romance in the air.

The next day there were recriminations and rumours
we weren't meant to hear. They drank strong black coffee
at Finnegan's, a blanket of smoke hanging heavy overhead,
while we, bored, stared at posters on the wall, Rheingold Girls
and the Yankees, Roger Maris and Mickey Mantle, or, ignored,
slipped outside to look at the boat, waiting for the clouds to lift.

Finally, there was the long trip home in the car, heading north
through diesel reek to a place where there were no bars,
only genteel drinks behind closed doors, and no boats,
no sea, only green pastures and trees, and in the back seat
we would sit in sullen silence, sucking salt from our hair
and dreaming of an island romance, of boats, and bars.

Out of the Blue

The kind policeman, with his platitudes and his cups of tea,
stands large between you and the rest of the room,
shielding you from what you've already seen,
your wife as you found her at the foot of the stairs,
in pieces, wild-eyed, slack-jawed, stone cold,
an insane mistake that makes no sense at all.

With casual platitudes and lukewarm tea the policeman
stands firm, shielding you from what he knows and you do not,
a shock, he says, when it happens like this, out of the blue,
and you try to remember what he means, what is blue,
the sky above you, the water below, the small screen
of the mobile phone lying beside you on the deck of the boat,

the constant blue of messages never received, replies not sent,
three whole days without a word? The policeman twitches,
smiles with guarded kindness, as if your solitude were a crime,
the two of you, alone, your wife at home with her poems,
struggling with words to ward off her demons, you on the boat,
battling the elements, trying to get something back from life.

An accident, probably, the policeman says, without conviction,
as if he isn't sure himself, what is an accident and what is not
in the ambiguity of the empty space between ceiling and floor,
between sea and sky, a slip of the tongue, a map misread, time
miscalculated, and in an absence of just three days, a woman
might fall and die, a man might sail away and never return.

The policeman with his wounding platitudes and his bitter tea
relaxes his stance, letting you see it all, the blood on the floor,
the shattered glass, your wife's broken body; at least it's clear
no one else was involved, he says, as if all those years together
meant nothing, as if you were a stranger who has just appeared
out of the blue, except you both know it never happens like that.

They Had a Garden

There they go: the child rides about in the wheel-barrow now;
everything else is in the pram, everything they own.

They had a garden. It was their pride and joy.
Now they dig about in the verges and in the woods,

planting this and pulling that, as if the land were all theirs,
every bit of it, and not someone else's,

and the wee boy, sitting proud in the wheel-barrow,
waves his little hand at you, as if he were a king.

A Change of House

The bare walls, the hard floors,
the anonymous echoes of unfamiliar rooms,
a change of house, every few years, and every time
he promises himself this house will be a home,
as he begins, again, the task of transformation,
chooses for his own room magnolia paint,
the colour of glowing skin, the blush on a woman's cheeks,
colour that fades, over time, to desperation,
and for the boy's room, primrose, the bright yellow
of early spring blossom, so full of promise
yet soon scarred and scuffed by adolescent frustrations,
and while the son dutifully paints the walls, the father
hangs curtains, lays carpets, linoleum, arranges furniture,
damping dangerous echoes and smothering the past
with the trappings of an unlikely domesticity.

It never works. Before long,
the new becomes familiar and the familiar
reawakens the past, and in the layered silence
of the large empty rooms he hears again
the distant whisper of a conversation, her voice
and his, and in the twitch of a curtain he sees
the graceful fall of her skirt fluttering around her knees,
and in the mist on the mirror her face reflects his own,
and every day he sees that same trick of fate
in the face of his son, the boy growing older,
their world changing, even as the father imagines
that everything since the day she died has remained
the same, that time has merely stalled, and waits
at night in the dark emptiness of his lonely room
for life to begin again.

Breakdown

Those long trails of fire
streaking across the horizon – right away,
I knew that the sky was falling, breaking apart,
that it was the beginning of the end,
that dark September night.

Then came a storm, the late summer wind stripping the trees
of leaves and limbs, and amid the debris left lying
in the streets, amid the litter and the leaves and the limbs,
lay pieces of the sky, shreds of clouds flapping
like tattered newspapers, shattered stars sparkling
like broken glass, great blue chunks of the firmament
gleaming with the dull brightness
of dirty puddles after a rain.

We played outside afterwards,
as usual, shuffling through dying leaves,
jumping over puddles of sky, jinking and juking
through fallen clouds. Time passed; perception altered.
In the fading light you disappeared.

I called out for you, but the words I spoke
fell out of my mouth like tiny chunks of ice,
and melted away on the ground without a sound,
as if nothing I might say could have any meaning or reason
in a world without substance, without integrity,
where matter and antimatter had collided once too often,
where all that was true had been annihilated,
and all that remained was a lie.

The Dog-Wifey

Growling and barking, teeth snapping,
eyes wild and ears flattened,
they come louping along the road.
You have to trust them,
believe in them,
let them come.

She steals them, one by one,
your dog, my dog, she takes them home;
tame as you please they go with her,
our dogs never again seen, invisible,
living inside her garden, inside her head,
the dog-wifey and her angel dogs.

With their dogs and their guns,
their needles and their knives,
their threats and their warnings,
they want to frighten you,
your fear their strength,
your faith your strength.

Imaginary dogs, imaginary enemies:
believe in the tail that wags the dog,
that drives your bitterest enemy
into your welcoming arms.

Dundee Wedding

Like spent confetti the tattered petals of crocuses
litter the grassy banks of the city's roads,
scattered by a relentless wind.

Among the reeds that fringe the Tay
she lay, mud oozing through her toes,
a baby's head emerging through the blood.

At high tide the mud and the reeds are hidden
beneath the quicksilver gleam of a dead-calm river.
Deep down, the dark water washes away her tears.

The wedding never happened. You see her now
tip-toeing round at the back of the Overgate
wrapped in a plaidie and wearing no shoes.

Along the river side, broken-backed daffodils
nod their shredded heads, wiser now, after the fact,
their beauty fading fast, their time past.

Shallow Land

Four little girls, standing on a beach,
shallow water lapping over bare bony feet,
brassy curls bobbing stiffly in the breeze,
pink painted toenails winking through the foam,
skinny arms akimbo, heads tipped coquettishly,
little women, mannequins, winsomely posed
on a cold northern beach under a sulky sky,

and tucked up against the dunes, a woman,
stick thin, hollow-eyed, straw hair and sallow skin
fading into the marram grass and the sand,
butterfly hands fluttering over a tiny screen,
another world – far from this deserted beach,
this sullen sky – at her fingertips, the internet
with all its possibilities, its intimacy, its anonymity,

and patrolling the beach, an ugly brute of a dog,
egg-shaped head and mean little triangular eyes,
all muscle and teeth, puffed with power and pride,
protecting his patch from whatever dangers lie hidden
in the whispering grass and the sucking tide,
menacing anything that moves on the shore,
lunging at the water, growling at the sky,

as the girls, driven forward by the tide, drift apart,
their pretty faces darkening, their childish delicacy hardening,
water lapping relentlessly over their cold, numb feet,
while the dog, racing frantically round and round
in ever-diminishing circles, howls at the tide,
desperately defending what little is left
of his narrowing beach beneath a widening sky,

and the woman slips, imperceptibly, into sleep,
lying somewhere between the water's end
and the bottom of the sky, in that shallow land
where nothing matters but the anonymous intimacy
of the lapping of waves rising gently over her toes,
the insistent licking of a tongue between her legs,
and the brutal indifference of cold bare feet on her breasts.

The Neighbour's Buddleia

In a neighbour's garden a long-neglected buddleia
lies sprawled across the grass after a storm,
elegant and indignant as an inebriated debutant,
a heap of leafy petticoats and pendent blossoms up-turned,
slender roots still clinging petulantly to sodden earth.

Nothing was ever quite right there.
The sagging roof, the zig-zag cracks in the harling
that no amount of paint could ever disguise,
the gate that squeaked at night, too often and too late;
so many small deceptions, such great aspirations.

Their one big moment was the garden party at Holyrood:
a chauffeur-driven limousine arriving at their gate,
your woman a vision in pistachio and white,
spikey heels and a too-wide hat,
wasp waist and spindle shanks.

Months later now, and that buddleia is still lying there,
brown leaves shrivelling, falling into the long grass,
the thin sapless limbs, hard as tines, uselessly forking the air,
a blowzy old bush, longing to be remembered
as the beauty they once believed it was.

The Marvel of the Parish

She thought no one would ever know. The marvel of the parish,
she hid her sins behind a camouflage of charity and good deeds,
and no one quite believed that her little acts of evil
had ever really happened; excuses were made.

Pain-stakingly, she sewed and crocheted
cloths for communion. Into every stitch
went avarice, spite, arrogance, pride,
and every possible unkindness.

When she died, blind eye was turned to blind eye
at the graveside in a pouring rain. Over that grave,
with evil leaching like a poison from the corpse,
no grass ever grew. God knew, if no one else ever did.

The Christian Door

A Christian door, your mother called it,
and you bowed your head before the cross
formed by the muntins and rails
of a door kept closed more often than not.
There was something sacred, you imagined,
in the secrets of that forbidden room –
the stifled whispers, the shuffle of sheets,
the creak of a bed-spring in the night –
and something of heaven and hell
in the storms that blew open the doors
with bright peals of laughter
or the shrill fury of angry words.

The barn, dark and cold and silent,
was a more pagan place, where dumb beasts,
amid blood and manure, silage and hay,
were born and died. The barn door,
heavy and hard to pull on its rusted rails,
was never closed, until that summer day
when you found it nearly so, and slid inside
to find your father dangling from a beam
with swallows buzzing round his head.

In the swallows' taunting chatter
you heard your mother's mocking laughter;
in the dark silence of the barn
you heard the whispered secrets of the bedroom.
The cross on the door was a coincidence,
a chance arrangement of pieces of wood,
nothing more, Christian only a word,
the sacred and the profane all the same.

The New Toboggan

Remember the snow, glittering blue-bright under a cold sun,
and the shivering children, giddy with anticipation,
screaming and shouting, their excited voices
shrill and sharp in the chill winter air;

remember their cries growing louder, more determined,
their bright smiles stiffening in the unforgiving cold,
their excitement waning, every attempt a failure,
the sleek new toboggan too long, unwieldy,

the snow too deep, too heavy,
the slope not as steep as we had imagined
yet still a hill, a burden to climb,
time after time, dragging the toboggan behind;

remember the hard edge of your stiff rubber boots
chafing against your calf, the icy burn of wet snow
on exposed ankles and wrists, feet and hands numb,
your body stiff, paralysed with cold;

remember standing alone, wanting to go home,
watching, as one last time they trudge back up the slope
and climb aboard the wooden plank, finally,
this time – without you – getting it right,

the toboggan gliding downhill, straight and true and fast,
a misty plume of snow rising proudly over the bent-wood bow,
then settling like diamonds on their woolly hats,
the wet snow blinding their eyes, freezing their frenzied cries;

remember a sudden cheerful exhilaration of blood
splattering the scene, a broken nose, a stunned silence,
the blooded victim stumbling home, screaming,
the others, frightened, scattering, embarrassed;

remember being abandoned, forgotten, standing alone,
idly flapping the reins of the disgraced toboggan,
admiring the tiny drops of blood, warm and fresh,
small red berries, sinking slowly into the cold white snow.

Milkweed Down

That morning the children were playing in the pasture,
pulling the ripening milkweed pods apart
to set the downy seeds aloft.

Alone in the kitchen their mother drank bitter coffee
and padded softly from room to room, her bare feet
sliding carelessly over a splintering floor.

Behind every passing car on the road a cloud of dust rose
and settled again, rank with the urban smells
of diesel and temptation.

Beside the house, clothes were drying on a line,
worn sheets and frayed towels, speckled brown
with floating milkweed down.

A haze formed over the sun in the deadening heat,
the soft morning hardening into afternoon,
the clothes wilting in the sun.

The children edged ever closer to the river's edge,
their parched heads and spindly limbs
thirsting for a swim.

A wind blew the milkweed seeds against the window
and in his delirium the children's father imagined sand
swirling in a desert storm.

Then the day exploded with thunder and lightning and rain.
The children ran home and stood shivering in the kitchen,
dripping rain and tears on the floor.

Their father, trembling in bed as his wife stroked his head,
dreamed of the sudden chill of the desert at dusk
and the comfort of a night with no end.

His wife kept an eye on the morphine, and spent the night
plucking milkweed seeds from the children's clothes
and splinters from her toes.

Earthquake

Perhaps it was the crowing of a cock that woke me,
or the honking of horns over the constant roar of traffic,
a morning like any other, noise never-ending in Mexico city.
You slept soundly, as if nothing could ever happen.

I couldn't understand how you could sleep like that.
I was raised on fear and terror, on warnings and threats.
Danger was everywhere. My family never slept
and always kept one eye on the door, every sense alert.

We had gone to a *bris* the day before, a family affair –
your family, not mine. The men had drunk good whisky
to settle their nerves, (though the father, your brother,
was afterwards rather green in the face, for quite some time),

while the women, stiff with hairspray and heavy with gold,
babbled careless vapidities and eyed one another's clothes
with open avarice, and the older ones spoke only Ladino,
to hide their unkind words from my ears, I imagined.

I have always imagined the worst; it's easier that way.
They would have seen the fear that I wear
wrapped about me like an old worn overcoat,
a dirty secret I couldn't possibly hide.

A cock crowing, cars honking, whatever: something woke me.
I left the bed, went to the window to inspect the day,
taking nothing for granted, looking for vital changes
in a city where nothing ever remained the same.

The Hasidim were leaving their homes, tidy and smart
in their hats and curls, as joggers ran laps around the tiny park.
I envied the joggers for their diligence, the Hasidim
for their faith, their customs, their daring to be different.

I turned away from the window, and noticed the paper lampshade
swinging gently in an imperceptible breeze. Dizziness and fear
made me weak at the knees. Nothing was as it seemed.
Somehow I had never imagined that was how it would be.

I stood in a door-way, as you had told me to do,
although I didn't believe it would do the trick,
and I left you there asleep in the bed;
as good a way to die as any, I supposed.

I could always imagine worse things;
certain things, I don't even have to imagine.
I know the worst; it's in my blood,
and nothing I do can ever change that.

In the kitchen a pot fell from the stove with a clang;
there were bangs, rattles, shuffling noises.
You tossed uneasily, but never woke
until just after the shaking had stopped.

'Earthquake,' you said, smiling at me where I stood,
as if it hadn't occurred to you that you might have died,
or that I might have tried to wake you to save your life;
in your eyes there was only unquestioning kindness.

I didn't want kindness; I didn't want your trust,
if that was what it was. Trust is fatal. 'Good-by,'
I said, although I couldn't tell from the way you smiled
if you understood that I was leaving for the last time.

Inheritance

The nights are long, the sun setting even as it rises,
the day gone by almost before it begins,
the darkness inside your heart, complete.

Alone in the house you roam from room to room
isolated behind closed curtains and locked doors,
your world shrinking in the lengthening nights.

He never bothered with his spectacles, or the details,
and missed, always, or dismissed, the finer points.
No one ever said, take a closer look; no one ever dared.

An insolent wind drives a hard rain against the windowpanes;
cold air slices knife-sharp through the gap in the curtains.
You pace the floor, waiting for spring.

One by one he took the pictures from the wall,
and placed them all, face down, on the floor,
the debris of a life misunderstood.

Outside, footsteps rustle through fallen leaves; all that money,
lost. Inside, you trample through the broken glass,
so many small details, gone forever, never missed.

In the lengthening days you glory in all you have left,
the promise of a butterfly's unexpected kiss,
the innocent sweat of rain in summer.

The Anarchy Waltz

for Nick Lunan

Anarchy was what you wanted, you always said.
I couldn't give you that.

Little tempests were the best I could do,
upside down mornings, and days that darkened
abruptly, and long, long nights,
filled with imperceptible absences,
a beat missed, now and then,
seven bars in an eight bar measure
that left you reeling,
one leg spare.

Still, we danced, me always on the left foot,
you on the right.

And here we are, still lurching round the kitchen at dawn,
out of step with everyone else, you always stirring,
burling me faster than I want to go
and laughing when I fall, both of us
out of control, wild,
inventing life, day by day,
the anarchy waltz
in real time.

Love at the Endings

She played the fiddle with an impossible stillness,
a shower of notes cascading from a nearly static bow.

Everything she did was subtle, unremarkable, quiet,
every movement she made almost invisible.

He longed to be in love with her, but had no idea where to begin.
Slowly, note by note, she reeled him in.

Then he discovered what those who knew the music
had always known: that there was a fire within her,

that the stillness masked a dangerous flamboyance,
a finely-tuned anarchy, a talent about to explode.

He learned to listen for the cracks in the music:
the misplaced notes, the missing beats,

the reel unravelling in subtle defiance of custom,
every stray note taking her farther away from him.

Now all that remains is an impossible stillness,
the thread of a melody with no beginning and no end.

Letters from a Lover Who Doesn't Exist

You do exist; we met, in a dark crowded room, a sweat
of moisture glistening nervously on cold walls, a thick mist
of insincerity masking dagger eyes and grovelling tongues,
impossible, there, to know what was real and what was not.

Nothing was said, that night, about the wife I knew you had,
or about the much younger woman at your side, and I knew,
in an instant, what sort of man you were, and kept my distance,
the threat of inconstancy chilling the air between us.

Letters arrive; you exist, but in another dimension, not mine.
I can't believe in you, any more than I can ever be certain
of what happens while I sleep, any more than I can measure
the depth of a shadow or the passing of time.

Like an injured bird left to recover alone in the dark,
your letters are lying in a box on a shelf, and I imagine,
at times, that I hear a rustling in the box, the scratching
of a pen, shadows rising from the dead, time, running out.

One day I will open the box and find that the letters
have vanished, nothing left but an untidy nest of dried ink,
a few threadbare words, a hard little nugget of spent affection
as indeterminate and unqualifiable as a cuckoo's egg.

Spring in the Glen

Spring was late coming to the glen;
not a bit of green to be seen
beneath the leaves lying dead on the ground,
and on the hills the grass was pale as mustard,
the bracken brown, the snow a cold and bitter blue.

She raked the ashes, plucked lumps of coal,
whole, from the spent fire: black the coal,
grey the ash, black her spirit,
silver-grey the strands in her hair
shining proud among the brown.

In the trees the rooks built their nests,
twigs dropping from their chattering mouths.
For kindling wood she stole their twigs;
with their raucous chatter they stole her sleep.

He might one day come to the door,
snow in his beard, tears in his eye,
his fingers frozen solid round his crook,
the one that was lost returned to the flock.

Beneath the trees a fallen rook danced, dazed,
crazed by the cold, black wings flapping,
grey beak frantically tapping
at the frozen earth.

The cat prowled with cunning patience,
his silver-black mackerel-striped back
weaving snake-like through the woods,
feigning indifference to the dying bird.

If her man returned it would be too late.
Nothing was the same. Promises made
were broken – his, to her; the laird's,
to his tenants; hers, to God.

She cared no more for the one that was lost
than she did for the other ninety-nine –
let them all die, out there on those cold blue hills,
believing, if they would, in the old certainties.

She had a fire to tend. Flames were rising,
sparks flying from the burning wood,
the coal, the papers, the books:
everything she had, she burnt.

Spring that year came late,
and when every stream was in spate
one last time she raked the ashes in the grate,
gave the cat a farewell clap,
and turned her back forever on the glen.

Stag

You the stag, lying wounded in the bracken,
weak, defenceless, dying: this is how it begins.

For you I would do anything, although I know
what little I can do will never be enough.

The ground between us is wet, the road rough,
I too long unaccustomed to this terrain.

Once I knew this peat bog well, cut this turf
long since, my sweat staining the damp dark earth.

You raise your head, shake your crown of horns,
eye me with disdain. I can smell your contempt.

You sense danger, stand proud to face the enemy.
Guided by you, I have lost my way.

The first shot fells you. 'That old rogue,'
the gillie crows. 'Never anything but trouble.'

A second shot stings my cheek; my blood rains red
over the boggy peat. 'Collateral damage,' the gillie says.

The Screen Door

He stands on the doorstep, head bent beneath a burning sun,
overcome by the sweet scent of incipient decay, of lost youth
and fading beauty, of privilege squandered and abused.

All that money, gone, nothing left of it now but the eye
on the dollar bill, a truncated pyramid, in God we trust, all of it
coming home to roost. Trust no one, someone told her once.

He strokes the knot of his tie, considers the spent blossoms,
the waste, the loss. Beside the house, the dry bed of a brook,
drained by drought and greed, reminds him of his mission.

Through the screen she sees a black suit, a tie, dark hair,
the eye on the dollar bill. From behind the screen she speaks;
'go away,' she should say. Instead she says, 'Come in.'

One false step, and it will all fall apart. They both know that.
The screen door is rusting, the paint peeling from the frame;
he would almost rather remain on the outside, looking in.

The hinges squeal as the door opens; a cat runs outside.
She hides her face behind her hair. 'I won't lie to you,'
he says, as if she had imagined he would. 'Trust me.'

You have to believe in the truth, and truth is all he has to offer.
He waits on the step as the door closes, not trusting himself,
studying her through the sienna haze of the rusted screen.

'This is all I have' she says. What if he says she is beautiful,
even now? She pats her wiry hair. Nothing will change.
The cat returns, scratches impatiently at the door.

He strokes his jaw, waits while she lets the cat back in.
He envies the cat, cradled now in her arms, so trusting,
despite all her excesses, the greed, the decay.

He came here to save her, she knows that, but there is no need.
Nothing will ever be the way it was; the tip of the pyramid
can never be replaced. Only the eye, ever watchful, remains.

'This is all I am,' he says, reaching out to stroke her hair.
His hand strikes the screen between them, and bleeds,
his thin skin shredded by the broken wires.

The School-Teacher's Wife

1 A Myre in Winter

Obsidian eye, gleaming in the pale winter light,
a myre in a forest of pines, slick with thin ice
splintered near the shore, where coot and moorhen
patter and splash through a slime of frozen weeds
and, ruffled, frightened by your approach,
hoot in warning; here, drawing near to the water's edge
you stop to stare, despairing, into that dark, unforgiving eye,
remembering his eyes, cold and black, his frosty breath,
a scent of cigarettes, the smell of semen and spruce,
the chill of winter air biting at your naked legs,
your back driven hard against the piney floor,
craving more, a word or two or a whisper beneath the trees,
the sweetness of a kiss – anything
to wash away the bitter taste of shame.

2 Sweeney Visits the Myre in Spring

I am Sweeney, and I am here.

Poor Sweeney, they say,
away with the drink. I say,
God bless the drink.
I couldn't live without it.

Reeds, thick now with rushy nests;
squalling gulls cluttering up the air –
under all that mess of nests
a woman lies dead.

Her body was never found.
She drowned herself;
only Sweeney knows where.

Clatter and chatter – these damn birds
never give a man a chance to think.
They say Sweeney talks too much.
Nobody wants to listen.

I saw a gull steal a chick
right out of the nest, and eat it.

'They even eat their own eggs,' she said.
'How do they ever survive?'
She was the school-teacher's wife,
a quiet woman with lonely eyes.

I've seen worse
I could have told her.

They always look the other way and say
'Poor Sweeney. Who knows what goes on
in that madman's mind?'

'Mister Sweeney,' she said.
She looked me in the eye.
'Good-by.'

I curse the day I came to live here
among these Scotchmen with their dirty way
of never saying what they have to say
to your face.

'Don't buy Sweeney a drink,'
they say. 'You'll never get away.'

Father Pat was for sending me home.
'You'd be better off,' he said, 'among your own.'

It was the potatoes that brought us here,
though there never was much money in tatties.
It was a chance to get away,
a way to get ahead.
All together we came,
men, women and children.
There's none of them left, now, but me.

I am Sweeney, and I am here.

There's the sun; oh, the heat of it!
Never a hint of rain today.
It's not all bad here,
not always all that bad.

I've seen people huddled together
like cattle in a shed,
the floor for a bed,
the rats in our hair,
the fire bursting out of straw,
the rush to the door,
the scorch of human flesh.
It was one of us, a man from home,
had locked us in. On his death bed
he confessed, said he'd only done
what he'd been told, just doing his job.
A man has to live. Now I'm alone;
it's only me that's left.

Fire in the water;
fire on the tongue.
The way the sun shines over the water
you'd think you could see her
down there where she lies
among the reeds.

Father Pat thought the cure at Lough Derg
was what was needed, St. Patrick's Purgatory
the very place for poor Sweeney.

I didn't mind it. I liked the silver water
and the swans. At night
my thoughts flew west
to the place where I was born
on the wild Atlantic shore.

But, you know, I never took the cure;
Lord love the drink,
whisky and beer my only companions.

I am Sweeney, and I am here.

Poor Sweeney, they say,
away with the drink.
They never listen!

I've seen the farmer's son
when he was young
taking eggs from the nest.
I've nothing against him now, though,
no matter what they say.
There's things I could tell them,
but nobody wants to hear.

He comes with a gun, and waits
beneath the pines. They say,
she ran away. I watched her go.

Only Sweeney knows where she lies,
and I'll never tell.
Nobody ever listens
to poor Sweeney.

Young Rankin the farmer's son
keeps his eye on the water,
his hand on the gun.
He'll shoot anything that moves, they say.

'I am Sweeney' –
calling like a madman
across the water,
my tongue on fire,
the fire in the water –
'Here I am!'

3 The School Teacher's Endless Summer Days

Silence, and heat – the long summer days begin
and never seem to end. No one speaks:
not a word. The children play their raucous games,
roaming freely through the streets, unafraid.
He hides, defeated, among the trees,
pacing a forest road beneath a sullen sun
hanging stagnant in the summer sky.
Dry the sandy soil, the sunburnt pines,
the thirsty weeds dying round the parched banks
of the shrinking myre: the driest summer in years.
Dry his eyes, his heart, his mind.
No farewells, no regrets, no tears.
She left, and never said a word.

The stifling silence, and the heat, and all this light:
the days begin and never seem to end.
The children play their careless games
mindlessly in the empty streets.
He knows their dark faces intimately –
the shallow hopelessness
of their blighted, ignorant lives.
He did what he could for them,
gave all he had to them.
He always thought she understood.

The silence, and the light, and the heat, clinging
like an unwanted embrace – the days begin,
and go on and on, every day the same.
Nothing ever changes.
The willowherb replaces the fading broom –
small changes, perhaps; he never noticed.
Their faces haunt him, every face the same,
the hollow, hungry look of the unenlightened.
He did what he could for them,
tried hard to change their lives for them.
Let them be, she warned him;

they never wanted change, she knew,
never shared his dream.
The children play dully in the stifling heat,
unafraid, his tyranny diminished in defeat.
They never speak to him,
but among themselves they whisper:
how could a man lose his wife?

A woodpecker's laugh breaks the lingering silence;
the flash of a jay streaks swiftly through the woods.
Time passes. He paces slowly along the forest road,
the earth baked hard beneath his feet.
His heart hardened, he waits only for September:
the dark classrooms, the shortening days, the helpless faces.
The children play frantically now, angry and afraid;
why must summer always come to an end?

4 Eclipse: The Farmer's Son Hunts Duck in Autumn

Eclipse: as dull as the duck, the drake
after breeding. Her word, eclipse; not mine.
I only know what I can see. This tree
she called an alder, its leaves in November
falling, all together, still summer-green.
Deciduous, she said, of the larch, as the needles
tarnished from green to gold and carpeted
the forest floor with an ochre mist.
Under Sitka spruce in the green darkness
we lay; she had a name for everything.

These teal in eclipse, stripped of colour,
look every one the same: no green,
no rust, on the head, no cream at the tail
to tell the female from the male, although to me
that doesn't matter much; I only know
what I can see. Easy prey, these little teal,
flitting playfully between the reeds;
it would please the old man to see me
dragging home a handful of feathery corpses,
something to show for all the hours
I've wasted here among the trees.

Hours, days, years – time means nothing to me.
I only know what I can see, and only these creeping shadows
mark the passing of time, as day darkens into night,
and only the changing light reminds me
of the passing of the seasons, a year now,
nearly, since we lay here among the pines.
But the old man says I'm wasting my time.
He wants me to be there with him, at home,
working hard on the farm. Hard work
without reward – that's all the old man knows.
The farm, when he's gone, goes;
there's nothing in it now but debt,
mortgages and loans, money spent long ago

before it was ever earned. 'And here's you,'
is all he says, 'Out shooting birds, all day long.'

Dunce, they called me at school,
the teacher the only one who ever understood
that words for me were no good. He put a pen in my hand
and told me to draw whatever I could.
I drew the myre's black eye and filled it in with ink;
overhead I drew the birds, every one,
as I saw them then, unique.
Drawing came easily to me, as easy as speech
to anyone else; easy to create the image of a bird,
the illusion of a bird, the memory of a bird,
but all I ever wanted was the vision of a bird: to see.

Harder, now, in this darkening light to see
these tiny teal, that flash of green
pretty on their wings as suddenly, from the water,
they rise and take flight, startled by some –
o*ne* – thing; Sweeney – *two* – it might have been –
three! I thought I caught a glimpse of his wild hair
and the mad glint of his wandered eye,
over there on the myre's far side.

Somewhere in the pines they fell, those duck;
with luck I'll find them all in this dim light.
A bat, blind, flaps past my head;
they see with their ears, she said, whispering softly
as we lay hidden in the trees, here where one teal
lies dead, blood running from the neck –
speak to me, she said, undressing.
The curve of her breast, the dark hollow
between her legs – groping in the shadows,
another teal here; I only know it by the feel
of wet flesh. Darkness closing in; of her
there's nothing left, only a memory,
and memories, like words, and time,
mean little to me – I only know what I can see.

The light now gone completely, I'll leave behind
the third bird where Sweeney will find it.
Only Sweeney knows where she is,
but no one ever listens to him.

A Distant Island

It seems as if the distance is greater now than once it was,
between that island, that little lump of banded gneiss
and vanished trees, and this unsteady shore.

Back when everything was close, I stood in a crowded bus,
flesh pressed against flesh, the hands of strangers
straying over my hips, the warm breath of a whisper
moistening my neck. 'Come,' you said.

It might be the island that is moving further out to sea,
or the shore receding, as if there had been a disagreement,
the one so steady and firm, the other, inconstant.

And now there is only this impersonal distance, a thumb
pressed against the soft resistance of a plasma screen
or a hand splayed over stuttering keys, one finger
hovering, always, over 'delete.'

Or is it that nothing at all has moved, yet the distance
between island and shore has grown: an illusion,
a lack of perspective, a trick of the imagination?

It is too far from me now, wherever it is, that little island
with its memory of trees and its elegantly folded rock.
Only a stray breath of wind can bring you back to me,
and only my faltering hand can breach the distance.

Acknowledgements and Notes

Thanks are due to the editors of the following publications, in which some of these poems were first published: *Acumen, Agenda, Crannóg, The Frogmore Papers, Gutter, The Interpreter's House, Northwords Now, Oasis, Orbis, Other Poetry, Pennine Platform, Poetry Salzburg, Poetry Scotland, The SHOp, Stand, Stony Thursday, The Warwick Review*, and the *Words on the Waves Award Anthology*.

At Meroe
For information about Meroe and about travel in Sudan, I would like to thank the Garstang Museum of Archaeology (University of Liverpool), David Smith, correspondent for the *The Guardian*, and June Eve Arbor, intrepid traveller.

The Baltic Shore
In January, 1945, 7,000 prisoners of war were marched by the SS from a prison in Konigsberg (now Kalingrad) to the Baltic Coast. At Palmnicken, (now Yantarny, Russia), they were herded into the sea and shot from behind.

One Day in Brussels
On 24 May, 2014, a gunman opened fire outside the Jewish Museum of Belgium in Brussels. Four people died.

Hector MacDonald in Paris
For information and details about the life and death of Hector MacDonald, my principal sources were *Fighting Mac: The Downfall of Major-General Sir Hector*, by Trevor Royle, and *Eachunn nan Cath*, by Ailean Friseal.

Carmichael in St. Kilda
The Gaelic phrases in this poem are taken from songs once sung in St. Kilda. For this poem and also the other poems about St. Kilda in this I collection, I am grateful to Roger Hutchinson, Donald Meek and Donald S Murray, all of whom have

challenged the prevailing myths about the history of the archipelago in their own writing.

The Innocents
This poem was inspired by eyewitness accounts of mass executions by the SS of Jews and Roma in the former Soviet Union. The accounts were collected by Yahad – In Unum, a global humanitarian organization founded by Father Patrick Desbois, and can be found on their website.